SALEM INTERIORS

The Southwest Parlor—RICHARD DERBY HOUSE—(1706-62)

Salem Interiors

TWO CENTURIES OF
NEW ENGLAND TASTE
AND DECORATION

Illustrations and Text by
SAMUEL CHAMBERLAIN

HASTINGS HOUSE, *Publishers* NEW YORK 22

THE PEIRCE-NICHOLS HOUSE

COPYRIGHT, 1950, BY SAMUEL CHAMBERLAIN   PRINTED IN THE UNITED STATES OF AMERICA

FOREWORD

The New England way of life, from the first epic days at Plymouth down to the present, has been pictured in many ways and in every recent decade. Novelists and historians have dwelt upon this rich theme at length. It has inspired poets, painters, and illustrators. That newcomer among the arts, photography, also finds here a fertile field for its graphic potentialities. The observant lens has created a vivid picture of our New England ancestors through the medium of the cinema. The still camera, in its quiet and inquisitive way, can choose several approaches in portraying the adventurous energy, the primitive hardships, and the fundamental good taste of the early American. One of these approaches is to cross the threshold of his own house, and to observe at close range his preferences in domestic architecture, in furniture, and the amenities of life. Such a procedure is adopted in this book.

Only a few cities provide sufficient background for this revealing study of early interiors. Boston, Providence, Portsmouth, New Hampshire and Salem, Massachusetts, are among them. Each can claim a few 17th-century wooden houses, several notable colonial dwellings with Georgian panel-ing, and plentiful three-story Federal mansions. But two things set Salem apart from the others. First of all, its houses often retain intact the furnishings of the original builders. For decades Salem was the great American seaport. Her merchants and sea captains made fortunes in the golden era of Yankee shipping. They retired early from their hazardous profession, built impressive houses, and installed in them the furniture, paintings, and china which they had acquired on voyages to Europe and the Orient.

Salem is unique in a second respect. It was the home of Samuel McIntire, America's greatest architural wood carver. The skill and subtlety of this gifted architect-craftsman, who was inspired by the Brothers Adam but still remained a creative genius in his own right, had a lasting effect on American decoration. Salem had an almost complete monopoly on his work. The rare privilege of reproducing many McIntire originals comes with the choice of Salem as the characteristic cross section of New England life and taste.

To obtain this illustrated narrative, some fifty-two historic Salem houses were photographed, with the permission of the owners. The written comment which accompanies the pictures is based on information generously supplied by these owners and on data available in the Essex Institute. The facts have been checked carefully, and it is hoped that no historical errors have appeared in this final draft.

It should be emphasized that these pages do not embrace *all* of the fine Salem houses by any means. The subject is too extensive and 176 pages are far too few. However, *most* of the famous houses are represented. Among them are about a dozen particularly fine ones which are open to the public, and so described in the captions. Due to the cooperation of other owners, we have been privileged to portray many fine rooms which are never open to public scrutiny. As a consequence, this book has the dual opportunity of serving as an informal guide to Salem's "open houses," and of providing new and unpublished glimpses beyond the thresholds of old private mansions.

The houses are presented in approximate chronological order, and indexed alphabetically on the last page. They begin with the Pickering House, dating from 1651, and end with the Victorian parlor of the Daland Mansion, built in the middle of the 19th century. They fairly and accurately represent two centuries of New England taste and decoration. Dates are not always easy to determine or to verify, so the word "approximate" must be emphasized.

The development of the New England house, from crude pine-sheathed rooms built around a mammoth fireplace, to lofty, mirrored 19th-century salons can be followed in this panorama of interiors. Much of Salem's early history is also reflected, although none of its houses, naturally enough, dates back to the days of Roger Conant, who arrived in this spot just six years after the landing in Plymouth. There is, however, a dramatic reminder of the witchcraft delusion of 1692, the most publicized and the least eradicable event in Salem history. This is the restored "Witch House" where Judge Jonathan Corwin lived and held preliminary hearings of persons accused of witchcraft. The John Ward House and the Hathaway House, both from the 17th century, are rare examples of the steep-gabled dwelling with an overhanging second story. So is the House of Seven Gables, which will always be associated with Salem's Nathaniel Hawthorne and his immortal novel.

The more developed architectural style of the 18th century is expressed in the noble Cabot-Endicott House and the brick residence of Richard Derby. Facing famed Derby Wharf, the latter was the finest of its time and a fitting symbol of the success of colonial traders and sea captains. But the great era of Salem shipping lay ahead. After the Revolution it expanded to dazzling proportions, creating fortunes for the intrepid young men who had the gift of seamanship—and salesmanship. An era of unprecedented building was the result. Three-story mansions with graceful doorways and exquisite interior woodwork cropped up in abundance. Samuel McIntire made his appearance at this time. His influence was felt from the 1780's until his death in 1811, and long thereafter. The 19th-century houses illustrated in the later pages of this book reflect, almost without exception, the wealth, ambition, and acquisitive good taste of Salem's merchant shippers.

If there ever was a book compiled by co-authors, this is it. Practically all of the research, the routine assembling of the facts, and the paving of the way for the invading photographer was accomplished by my brisk but retiring wife, Narcissa G. Chamberlain. She rightly belongs on the title page, but prefers becoming anonymity. To her, and to the generous, cordial, and cooperative owners of the Salem houses illustrated on these pages, I beg to express warm and heartfelt thanks.

SAMUEL CHAMBERLAIN

The Pickering House

This venerable structure rightfully comes first in the imposing procession of historic Salem houses. Built by John Pickering in 1651, it has been owned and occupied by one family for ten generations. The building was originally a farm, known as "Broadlands," with some twenty-five acres of land. Many a shipmaster later built his mansion on lots bought from the Pickering farm. The Revolutionary hero, Timothy Pickering, was born in this house. After serving as a General during the War for Independence, he occupied high cabinet posts under George Washington and John Adams. The antiquity of the house is partially concealed by exterior changes made about 1841. The mood of that moment was to add wooden Gothic "gingerbread" trimmings. Few structures have survived this indignity with more poise than the Pickering house.

The east chamber of the Pickering house is furnished with original pieces, including a mahogany highboy and a venerable winged chair. The fireplace, of later date, is faced with old English tiles.

The parlor in the Pickering house holds to the "best front room" tradition. The walls are papered in white and gold. The mantel shelf glistens with crystal ornament and the sofas shine with gold brocade.

The lower hall. Over a century ago this passage was cut through the massive central brick chimney.

One of the most graceful pieces in the parlor is this mahogany Sheraton tambour desk.

This corner cabinet in the parlor displays a collection of old Lowestoft china which bears the initials of the original owners, Benjamin and Elizabeth Cox. The 52-piece set includes three helmet pitchers.

The library is the oldest part of the Pickering house. The present mantelpiece, though an old one, was doubtless built over a larger opening, with a massive oak lintel and brick ovens. Standing at the left is an Elizabethan table brought to this country from England in 1637 by the first John Pickering.

Original beams are exposed in the library and the woodwork is painted a soft green. The portrait of Mary Pickering Leavitt and her daughter is by Joseph Badger. An old milk bench serves as a coffee table.

The east chamber of the Pickering house is dominated by a noble four-post bed, at the foot of which is an old leather chest. Wallpaper and hand-hooked rugs adhere to simple and authentic patterns.

The canopy of the old field bed makes an intricate frame for the mantelpiece, where the combination of a formal acanthus leaf and an Ionic pilaster constitutes a pleasant breach of architectural propriety.

The west chamber is enlivened by a half-canopy bed which belonged to one of the children of Mary Pickering Leavitt. The hangings and bedspread are old ones, bordered with hand-made netting.

Between the windows of the west chamber stands a lowboy, flanked by Sheraton chairs. Braided oval rugs do not conceal the fine wide floor boards. Paneled shutters, which are plentiful throughout the house, show up well in this view. An old spinning wheel stands next to a "gunstock" post at the left.

THE STEPHEN DANIEL HOUSE. After many vicissitudes this 17th-century dwelling has recently been restored and opened to the public as a restaurant. It was originally built in 1667 by Stephen Daniel, mariner. Later, in 1756, a wing and third floor were added. In the dining-room stands this English oak dresser, dating from about 1700, and gleaming with old pewter. The pewter collection contains plates, two sets of matched mugs, coffee urns, pitchers, candlesticks, and a rare hot-water platter.

In the ancient kitchen of the Stephen Daniel house is a fireplace whose scarred oak lintel is liberally carved with initials. This corner of the fireplace is rich in the atmosphere of pioneer days.

The parlor of the Stephen Daniel house is in a later wing. The woodwork is painted a dull grey green. Above the mantel hangs a painting of the ship "Sea Lark" and two rare silhouettes by Peale and Brown.

The massive brick fireplace of the old kitchen is fitted with all of the necessary equipment for an early New England housewife, including a musket. The door at the left leads to a secret stone hideout.

The dining-room of the Stephen Daniel house is cheerful and inviting, especially when the sunlight pours through its west windows. The curtains are made of New England drugget, 125 years old.

Framed with simple paneling, the dining-room fireplace shares the same chimney with the old kitchen hearth, but is smaller in scale. The five-slat armchair is unusual, as is the towering old settle.

The House of Seven Gables

To the public at large, the best known of all Salem houses will always be this steep-roofed, almost Elizabethan structure, built in 1668 by Captain John Turner. After three generations of Turners had lived in it, the house was bought by the Ingersoll family in 1782. During the time that spinster Susan Ingersoll lived here, one of the few men allowed to cross the threshold was her cousin, Nathaniel Hawthorne, and it is a fair assumption that he had this house in mind when writing his great romance. The House of Seven Gables, the Hathaway house, and the Retire Beckett house form a group of three which are open to the public, for the benefit of social service work in the neighborhood.

The attic is as stimulating as the novel. Standing on the wide floor boards are two spinning wheels, an old model of the House of Seven Gables and a weathered piece of the original nail-studded door.

The fireplace of the old kitchen in the House of Seven Gables has a built-in brick oven with an early wooden door. On the mantel shelf stand old candle holders, irons, whale oil lamps, and a candle mold. On the hearth, among other articles, are two tin "kitchens" for roasting meat, foot warmers and stools.

Another view of the old kitchen reveals two ladder-back chairs, a venerable hide-covered chest, and a cupboard of early date. Thousands of visitors have signed the guest book on the desk at the right.

In the dining-room of the House of Seven Gables is a Hepplewhite sideboard and a William and Mary armchair where Dr. Pyncheon, in Hawthorne's novel, was found dead by the butcher boy. At the right is a "dinner wagon" and tray which belonged to Susan Ingersoll.

Among several pieces on the dining-room sideboard is a large Sheffield urn, partly silhouetted against an 1860 ship painting. The wallpaper is reproduced from an old Chinese pattern.

The ceiling of the parlor sags with age, but the room retains its dignity, as does the portrait of John Turner III, grandson of the builder. Furnishings include a Sheraton stand and chairs.

Fine paneling, with discreet pilasters and arched cupboard doors, graces the north wall of the parlor. Over the fireplace hangs a portrait of the daughter of John Turner III, Mrs. Daniel Sargent.

The parlor cabinet has a hand-carved shell back. On the scalloped shelves are fine pieces of Lowestoft.
Queen's ware, lusterware, and a Liverpool pitcher. The lower shelves hold pickle and ginger jars.

In the upstairs chamber, known as "Phoebe's Room" in Hawthorne's classic, hangs a portrait of Nathaniel Bowditch, Salem's great mathematician and author of *The New American Practical Navigator*. A Queen Anne mirror hangs over a fine early walnut chest of drawers. In the corner is a Queen Anne highboy.

Also in "Phoebe's Room" is a four-post bed which once belonged to the Hawthorne family.

In the novel, Hepzebah kept a "penny shop" in a small front room, and such a shop existed in Susan Ingersoll's day. Before that the room served as a toll house for the Salem-Marblehead ferry. In the present shop are bits of old china, prints, boxes, toys, and wooden jointed dolls in period costumes.

THE HATHAWAY HOUSE, built in 1682 and long known as "The Old Bakery," was rescued from the house wreckers in 1911 and now forms part of the House of Seven Gables group. This is the kitchen.

The walls of the old kitchen in the Hathaway house are partly covered with rough plaster and partly finished with vertical sheathing. The room contains a fine collection of 17th-century kitchen implements.

The John Ward House

This fine 17th-century gabled house was moved from its original site on St. Peter Street to the gardens of the Essex Institute in 1910. It has been restored and carefully furnished, and is open to the public during the summer months. The house dates from 1684. Among its curious rooms are a "cent shop," a weave room, an apothecary's shop, a restored kitchen, and a dining-room with a fine beamed ceiling. One of the rare houses with an "overhang" and Elizabethan gables, it was originally a small house, built around a single chimney. Later it doubled in size, and then a lean-to was added, an architectural progression common in early New England.

In the dining-room of the John Ward house stands an old gate-leg table, surrounded by William and Mary chairs. A cradle and a spinning wheel occupy traditional places before the fireplace, which is flanked by vertical sheathing. The original oak purlins and chamfered beams support the wood ceiling.

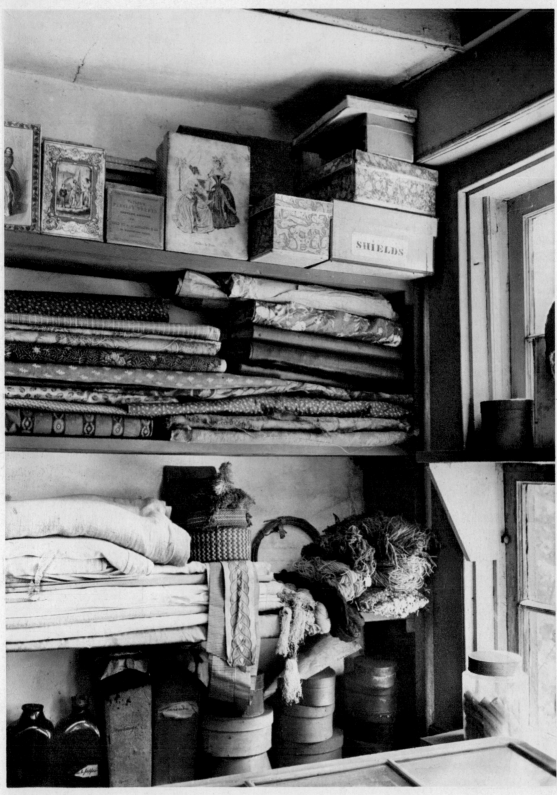

In the lean-to of the John Ward house is an early 19th-century "cent shop" whose shelves, laden with printed cotton lengths, yarn and ribbons, old boxes and bottles, look precisely as they did a century ago.

Children used to come to the "cent shop" to buy toys, peppermint drops, gingerbread men, "Gibraltars" and "Blackjacks" displayed in old showcases. Cotton prints and wool socks are festooned against the wall.

In the kitchen is a family table, set with wooden plates. Its hard stools were not made for comfort.

An apothecary shop of 1830, with jars, mortars, and old prescriptions, is also in the lean-to.

The kitchen of the John Ward house recreates the atmosphere of the 17th century down to the smallest wooden saltcellar. Wide horizontal sheathing cover its walls. Pewter and wooden plates rest on the table and pine dresser. The diamond-paned casements are copies of originals in the Essex Institute.

The kitchen fireplace is of brick, spanned by a heavy oak lintel, to which is attached an ingenious "jack" for turning the roasting spit. The brick baking oven has a removable wooden door. Adjoining it is a wooden bench for the colder winter evenings when the high-back settle was not warm enough.

Witch House

The City of Salem has often contributed to the preservation of its architectural treasures, a recent example being the restoration of the Witch house. At least a part of this picturesque structure was standing in 1675. For many decades it carried the silhouette of a gambrel-roofed house, but extensive research has convinced the experts that it originally was the many-gabled, almost Elizabethan house which now stands on Essex Street. Its name comes from the fact that this was the home of Jonathan Corwin, one of the judges of the witchcraft court. Some of the preliminary hearings in the witchcraft cases were held here.

An old loom has been installed in the east bedroom of the Witch house and now weaves as effectively as it did in the late 1600's. Before the fireplace stands an antique yarn reel.

The living-room of the Witch house is framed with fine solid beams. Some of the posts are carved in the familiar gunstock pattern. The fireplace lintel is bedecked with musket and powder horns, in the spirit of the times.

An impressive four-post bed, shrouded in white hangings, stands in a corner of the west bedroom.

This simple fireplace is flanked by an old Brewster chair and an early desk.

The Stearns-Sprague House

This is one of Salem's early 18th-century houses. It was occupied by the Spragues and their descendants, the Stearnses for ten generations. Built by Joseph Dean in 1706, it is better known today as the "East India House." Toward the end of the 18th century it was remodeled, and Samuel McIntire is known to have worked on the house at that time. He probably built the front porch.

A display of old guns, Burmese knives, tankards, and German helmets, lends character to one of the rear rooms of the Stearns-Sprague house.

The dining-room fireplace in the Stearns-Sprague house dates from about 1765 and may contain early McIntire woodwork. The marble mantel is of a later period and painted over.

In the paneled Red Room or salon the Spragues entertained General Lafayette. In the panel above the fireplace hang two exquisite French light-plaster medallions portraying Louis XVI and Marie Antoinette

The Louis XVI medallion.

The Marie Antoinette medallion.

The Neal House

Built by the Neal family in the early 18th century, this house is one of several which lends historic atmosphere to Broad Street.

The dining-room of the Neal house is distinguished by a wainscoting of horizontal panels, typical of the early 18th century. A simple drop-leaf table and Hitchcock chairs are quite at home in this setting.

The dining-room is low-studded and almost severely simple. Considerable warmth is lent by the painted woodwork, whose tone is a soft pale pea green.

Marine and flower prints brighten the walls, and silver sparkles on the lowboy.

A narrow bolection moulding frames the fireplace The panels above vary considerably in width.

The east bedroom of the Neal house contains a fireplace with sloping recessed sides. The paneling has been scraped down to reveal the natural pine. The sidelights are modeled after old candle sconces.

The mantel in the living room of the Neal house dates slightly after McIntire, and is painted black.

The south chamber contains a gun collection. Four Revolutionary muskets hang over the hearth.

The low-studded hall of the Neal house has many of the earmarks of a very early dwelling. A steep little stairway runs up beside a central chimney whose bricks are exposed on the hall side.

The Ropes Mansion

Preceded by a brick walk lined with statuesque wooden gate posts, this is one of Salem's most impressive houses. Built about 1719, it was purchased by Judge Nathaniel Ropes in 1768 and remained in the same family until 1907. The Judge was a strong Loyalist, and the house was attacked by angry patriots in 1774. Under the will of the last Ropes owners, the house and its well-kept gardens are now open to the public. As it stands, the house provides an accurate picture of the possessions and the way of life of a well-to-do Salem family in the early 19th century.

The Judge Ropes chamber is the best room in the house, containing several good pieces, among them a serpentine-front bureau dating from about 1750 and a most inviting early winged rocking chair.

The Judge Ropes chamber demonstrates how spaciousness and comfort can be combined with early New England simplicity. The window frames are unusually wide and contain finely built folding shutters.

The four-post bed in the Judge Ropes chamber dates from shortly after 1800, while the Queen Anne lowboy and mirror are from about 1720. The Chippendale chair is one of four in the room.

The most interesting exhibit in the Ropes mansion is the complete double set of Canton china which was imported for Sally Fiske Ropes at the time of her wedding to her cousin, Joseph Orne, in 1817. Along with fine Irish glass and other pieces, it is displayed in a special room. This view shows only a portion of the set. Sally Ropes died shortly after her marriage, and the china spent decades packed in barrels.

The Clark-Morgan House

This old gambrel-roofed dwelling is a most atmospheric reminder of early Salem. Built in the second quarter of the 18th century, it has four pedimented windows and a cheerful shuttered doorway facing the time-worn brick sidewalk on Essex Street.

The dining-room of the Clark-Morgan house is finished in a light turquoise blue, one of the authentic colors of the period. The mahogany lowboy from New Hampshire has a most unusual "bombé" design.

The living-room of the Clark-Morgan house is low-studded and paneled. The two front windows are curtained as one with red brocade. The Hepplewhite table is dominated by a very Gallic rooster.

Transformations are evident in the old kitchen, which now serves as a small dining-room.

The living-room fireplace in the Clark-Morgan house has the bolection molding and simple panels typical of the early 18th century. The mantel shelf, a later addition, holds a pair of three-branched candelabra with a Bacchic motif. The Chinese fan and porcelain jars were brought from China many years ago.

The Cabot-Endicott House

This large and dignified gambrel-roofed house on Essex Street was built in 1748 for Joseph Cabot. Its English architect is also supposed to have designed "The Lindens," originally built in Danvers. Judge William Crowninshield Endicott, Justice of the Supreme Court and Secretary of War under President Cleveland, later bought the house. Here he entertained General Sherman and the Right Honorable Joseph Chamberlain of England, who later married the Judge's daughter, Mary Crowninshield Endicott.

A wide, framed double door connects the drawing-room and the mirrored dining-room of the Cabot-Endicott house. In recent years the house has been carefully restored and furnished with period pieces.

The drawing-room of the Cabot-Endicott house has an air of cheerful dignity. The woodwork is painted white, and the fireplace is faced with yellow marble. Two rare silk embroideries hang framed on the wall.

The drawing-room is brightened by three large windows framed in gold brocade curtains. The rounded bay was added by the Endicotts and extends up two stories. The old armchair dates from about 1710.

The dining-room of the Cabot-Endicott house achieves distinction by the presence of high recessed windows and a good cornice. The dining-room mantelpiece is reflected in a formal 19th-century gilt mirror.

In the dining-room, a French foot American secretary, dating from about 1800, makes a handsome china cabinet. It is flanked by four old color prints, emblematic of England, Scotland, Ireland, and Wales.

The dining-room is also finished in white and gold, a luminous background for a Hepplewhite sideboard and matching chairs. Over the sideboard is a portrait of an early Salem sea captain, James Buffington.

The lower hallway of the Cabot-Endicott house is wide and hospitable. The stairway is one of the finest in Salem, leading majestically between rich balusters and a paneled wall to a lighted landing.

Each step of the hall staircase has three turned balusters of different length and design.

The newel post of the hall staircase is an intricate spiral. On the opposite wall is an Italian gilt mirror.

The library of the Cabot-Endicott house is a comfortable, high-ceilinged room with four windows. The mantelpiece is from a later period than the house itself, being reminiscent of McIntire's work.

A detail of the library mantel reveals garlands and reeding, and a slightly crowded wheat sheaf.

The landing of the stairway is lighted by a recessed arched window overlooking the garden.

The southeast bedroom of the Cabot-Endicott house has a flat paneled chimney-piece faced with tile. Traditional striped paper covers the other wall surfaces. The Sheraton four-post bed has a chintz canopy.

The southeast bedroom has a sunny three-windowed bay, corresponding to the drawing-room below. The chintz curtains match the bed hangings and the rug is Chinese, reproduced from an Aubusson design.

The northeast bedroom of the Cabot-Endicott house contains a fine maple field bed with an early netted canopy and knotted bedspread. The old winged chair belonged to the family of the present owner.

The paneled end of the northeast bedroom reveals graceful carving without elaboration. Over the fireplace is an old engraving depicting one of Benjamin Franklin's moments of social triumph.

THE LINDALL HOUSE, built in 1755, can well be proud of its ornamental stair rail with varying balusters and an intricate newel post which would do credit to a carver of ship models. Benjamin Thompson, later Count Rumford, lived here for three years. Better known as the Cook house, it now serves as headquarters for the Salem Chapter of the American Red Cross.

THE MACKEY-WHEATLAND HOUSE was built on Essex Street sometime before 1760. Three late 18th-century furniture designs blend well in its cheerful dining-room. As in so many Salem houses, the walls are enlivened with prints by Salem's great contemporary painter and etcher, Frank W. Benson.

The Hepplewhite sideboard is notable because of its small size. The card table is Sheraton.

A large oval gilt mirror hangs in the hall, silhouetted against a paper of Oriental inspiration.

Furniture in each corner of the dining-room forms a graceful composition. Here a stately chest-on-chest contrasts with the light grace of a piecrust table, with an inlaid rosette, and a mahogany lowboy.

The front living-room of the Mackey-Wheatland house is papered in Chinese silver and vermilion tea paper. The grey marble mantel is fitted with old brasses. Over it hangs a Frank W. Benson watercolor. The old secretary in the corner belonged to Augustus Perry, great-grandfather of the present owner.

The Eden-Browne-Sanders House

The Eden-Browne-Sanders house on Summer Street was built in 1760. The story goes that when it was finished the Eden family went up to the roof, taking a bottle of champagne with them, and christened the house "The Garden of Eden." Thomas Eden was a shipmaster, and his house was built by shipwrights. The ridgepole is said to be an inverted ship's keel.

The drawing-room of the Eden-Browne-Sanders house is low-ceilinged but spacious, furnished with old family pieces. In the far corner is a graceful and quite unusual Sheraton secretary.

The drawing-room of the Eden-Browne-Sanders house contains two identical fireplaces, one in the original part of the house and another in an extension added in 1814. The old tambour desk is noteworthy.

The north end of the drawing-room reveals 19th-century interior trim. The room contains two fine Duncan-Phyfe mahogany tables, one of which is shown at the left.

An old Franklin stove serves as a fireplace in the library of the Eden-Browne-Sanders house. The room is filled with maps, paintings, ship models, and memorabilia, including a large brass key, which once gave access to the warehouse of an early Salem shipmaster, and a Civil War sword.

The drawing-room and its two fireplaces, seen from the front hall.

The hall is brightened by Chinese paper, a fine stair rail, and, above the mirror, a fireman's helmet.

The north parlor of the Eden-Browne-Sanders house is small and intimate, centering about a fireplace whose mantel is in the best McIntire tradition. A model ship could hardly have a better background.

The lower-hall stairway may have come from England. Fan and side lights frame the doorway.

The upper hall reveals a rich architectural treatment with fine paneling—and the traditional clock.

THE PUNCHARD-DALAND HOUSE has undergone many changes since it was built by Benjamin Punchard, well before the Revolution. The present dining-room was once a "cent shop" on Federal Street, with a door between the windows. That space now has shelves displaying rose medallion china.

The living-room of the Punchard-Daland house may have been added in 1735, a date carved on a ceiling beam. The old paneling serves as a background for decorative Chinese pieces and a Chippendale chair.

In the living-room of the Punchard-Daland house is an exceedingly rare "florid type" chest. Carved by Thomas Dennis of Ipswich, and dated 1634, it has never left the present owner's family.

THE SANDERSON HOUSE, nearby on Federal Street, was built about 1781 by Elijah and Jacob Sanderson, who belonged to a flourishing family of Salem cabinetmakers. The dining-room contains an old bow-front Sheraton sideboard of unusual design. Above it is the portrait of Nancy Putnam, daughter of the famed Gideon Putnam of Saratoga Springs. The picture was painted by Nelson Cook in 1844.

A pair of old Windsor chairs flank the fireplace in the dining-room of the Sanderson house.

The hall staircase is richly paneled. At the landing hangs a rare mirror clock, made in Lowell.

The dining-room of the Sanderson house is simply paneled. Old ovens are hidden by a low cupboard door. The pair of candlesticks on the mantel shelf are old Sheffield, the rest of the objects pewter.

THE BOTT HOUSE, built in the late 18th century by James Bott, the saddler, is the oldest house on Salem's celebrated Chestnut Street. Nathaniel Hawthorne lived here for a time about 1847. The dignified drawing-room has a fine American Sheraton maple sofa, flanked by a pair of old tripod tables.

The drawing-room fireplace in the Bott house has typical early paneling without a mantel shelf.

The dining-room of the Bott house contains an unusually fine William and Mary walnut highboy.

The Richard Derby House

This, the oldest brick house in Salem, was built between 1760 and 1762 by Captain Richard Derby for his son, Elias Hasket Derby. It now sits serenely at the head of the once famous Derby Wharf. In 1927 it was rescued and restored by the Society for the Preservation of New England Antiquities. At present it is a part of the Salem Maritime National Historical Site, a notable project undertaken by the Department of the Interior.

The paneled interiors of the Derby house are among the most colorful which exist from this period. In this southeast parlor the woodwork is painted a rich olive green. A bannister-back armchair and a primitive reading stand sit near the window. Against the right wall is a desk-on-frame, dating from about 1700.

The olive green china closet in the parlor of the Derby house is enlivened with Delft plates, Bristol pitchers and glass jars, and pewter platters. At the left hangs a portrait of Elias Hasket Derby.

The dining-room of the Derby house is furnished with an early gate-leg table and a corner cupboard filled with Oriental and European ware. The woodwork is green. Against the oyster white plaster walls are old racks for spoons and clay pipes. The brass chandelier came from Holland about 1750.

Close examination of the paneled box stairway in the Derby house and the intricate turning of the bal-usters in three patterns reveals the full splendor of 18th-century craftsmanship in Salem.

On exhibit in the Derby house is a collection of old decorated tin pieces with their original designs.

In the southwest parlor is a noble chest of drawers from about 1650 with unusual openwork brasses.

This rare portable desk and "courting" glass occupy a corner of the blue bedroom.

Apple green is the color note of the southwest bedroom in the Derby house. The Queen Anne table and mirror harmonize well with the earlier ladder-back armchair. The candlesticks have scalloped bases.

A child's chair and toy cradle sit beside the fireplace in the southwest bedroom. The andirons are early and graceful. In contrast to the prevalent green, the bolection moulding is painted a brownish red.

In the northwest back bedroom of the Derby house the color becomes more pronounced. The woodwork is painted a dark blue green. The only paper in the house appears here, a reproduction of the original Chinese tea-box paper once used. The bedspread is a hand-stitched turkey-red homespun.

The woodwork in the southeast bedroom in the Derby house is finished in an old powder blue, contrasting happily with the white plaster walls. Near the fireplace is a Derby family cradle, made in 1735.

The blue southeast bedroom contains a fine mahogany broken-arch highboy. Beside it stands a Queen Anne chair. The four-post bed is covered with a colorful India cotton print bedspread.

THE CAPTAIN THOMAS MASON HOUSE on Cambridge Street was built in the last quarter of the 18th century. Its dignified, well-proportioned paneled rooms clearly reflect the Georgian influence.

A detail of the living-room mantel in the Captain Thomas Mason house reveals finely carved mouldings and a sentimental sculptured group of great charm. Successive coats of paint have somewhat dulled the contours of the gamboling cupids, their playful lion and their two lyric maidens.

The Peirce-Nichols House

Samuel McIntire's early masterpiece has often been characterized as the finest three-story wooden house in New England. Built in 1782 by Jerathmiel Peirce, wealthy ship owner and East India merchant, the house stands on Federal Street, serene behind its elaborate white fence, an eloquent symbol of Salem's era of shipping prosperity.

The plans of the house were McIntire's, and the wood carving, which took long years to finish, represents some of his finest handiwork. He also designed and built some of the furniture expressly for this house. For many years the house has been the property of the Essex Institute, and it is open to the public at certain hours each week. The principal front rooms have been restored and furnished with careful regard to authentic detail and atmosphere.

In the drawing-room is a decorative fireplace executed in McIntire's later Adamesque style. This room was remodeled by McIntire in 1801 on the occasion of the marriage of Jerathmiel Peirce's daughter to George Nichols. The mirror over the mantel was ordered from France at the time of the wedding.

This doorway and cornice in the drawing-room of the Peirce-Nichols house show the subtle delicacy of McIntire's style at its peak. Flanking the door are two of his own "cathedral-back" chairs.

A detail of the drawing-room mantel reveals McIntire's deft handling of classic architectural form.

The south end of the drawing-room is lighted by two large windows. The McIntire window seats, shaped to fit the sloping sides of the embrasures, are upholstered in soft blue and white satin stripe and finished with festoons of brass nails. Between the windows is another French gilt mirror of the period.

The mantel is flanked by two recesses, each containing a miniature McIntire divan. Other original pieces are grouped around the tea table. The woodwork is white; the wallpaper white with a gold pattern.

In the drawing-room is an old rosewood piano made by Clementi and Company of London in the early 19th century. Above it hangs a most engaging "Cupid on a Shell," painted by Vervoort and dated 1822.

The west parlor of the Peirce-Nichols house is an earlier room, distinctly Georgian in feeling. The walls are a soft cocoa color. The wide, well-polished floorboards add distinction to the room.

An earlier view shows the west parlor when it was embellished by a landscape paper. The old portraits are of an unknown lady and gentleman. A celestial globe stands near the serpentine-front desk.

Heavy Georgian mouldings and an ornamental band of grey Sadler tiles, depicting scenes from Aesop's *Fables,* frame the fireplace opening in the west parlor. The chairs are upholstered in the same shade.

The cupboard contains a collection of blue Canton china of the Fitzhugh pattern (1800-1810)

The wide doorway in the central hall is framed in exquisite carved detail embracing a fanlight.

The large east bedroom of the Peirce-Nichols house contains several fine pieces. Among them is a field bed, one of whose four carved posts appears in the foreground. The wallpaper repeats a vigorous historic design in soft blues. Through two McIntire doorways is a glimpse of the upstairs sitting-room.

The fireplace in the east bedroom of the Peirce-Nichols house is framed by two doors opening on ample wardrobe closets. In the framed panel are two American primitive gouache paintings.

The carver-architect introduces half-engaged columns and a panel of vertical reeding in the east bedroom mantel. The fireplace opening is brightened by a polished brass frame.

The four-post bed with netted canopy belonged to the Nichols family. The coverlet is of copperplate print. The camphor wood chest, leather covered and studded with brass nails, is also a Nichols piece.

Near the south window is a superb old block-front mahogany chest-on-chest with shell carving.

A detail of the Georgian mantel in the upstairs sitting-room shows red-orange Sadler tiles.

The hangings in the upstairs sitting-room reproduce an old pattern in tans and red. A delicate Sheraton sofa is placed near the fireplace, and on the wall is a banjo clock by Aaron Willard, Jr.

Fine paneling surrounds the fireplace of the upstairs sitting-room in the Peirce-Nichols house. Two venerable leather water buckets stand on either side of the iron grate, a 19th-century addition.

The Assembly House

This is one of the rare houses in Salem which was not originally planned as a private dwelling. Built in 1782 as a Federalist Club, it served for years as the setting for concerts, plays, oratorios, and dances. The Marquis de Lafayette attended a ball here in October 1784 and, five years later, George Washington was entertained in its candle-lighted salons. The building was remodeled as a private dwelling in 1796, receiving a cheerful new façade with Ionic pilasters. The grape-festooned portico was added after 1830. It is believed that Samuel McIntire undertook the remodeling, or at least had something to do with it. Although it has been a private residence ever since, the house still retains some of the atmosphere of a club, particularly in the stair landing and the fine old billiard room.

The parlor of the Assembly House is furnished with teakwood pieces brought from China, India and Zanzibar by one of Salem's early shipmasters. The curtains are black and gold brocade with gilt cornices.

The woodwork in the parlor of the Assembly House may well be the work of Samuel McIntire. In the reeded panel over the mantel hangs a portrait, painted on ivory, of Captain James Silver of the ship "Leander." Below the portrait, flanked by Chinese vases, is the alabaster bust of his son, Peter Silver.

The parlor of the Assembly House provides a Federalist setting for exotic pieces brought from the Orient, a phenomenon which often occurs in Salem mansions built by prosperous shipmasters and merchants.

On the teakwood stand is a carved elephant from a Hindu temple.

An extraordinary formal doorway, with a graceful bust in its broken pediment, is at the landing.

In the dining-room of the Assembly House restrained woodwork sets off the colorful hand-painted Chinese paper.

The Sheraton sideboard is an Occidental piece which goes well with an Oriental wall covering.

Over the dining-room doorway is a Chinese carving of a Phoenix bird.

The architectural treatment is rich in the lower hallway of the Assembly House, which once witnessed the arrival of many a distinguished Salem visitor. The doorway is unsymmetrically placed.

THE FRANCIS TUCKERMAN PARKER HOUSE, built on Botts Court sometime before 1800, contains exquisite Colonial furnishings, among them this unique girandole mirror

A Queen Anne lowboy stands beneath the girandole mirror in the living-room of the Francis Tuckerman Parker house. It was once known as "The House in the Marsh" when it stood on swampy land.

In the upper hallway stands a mahogany block-front chest-on-chest made by Abraham Watson.

A compact sea captain's desk occupies a corner of the living-room. Above it is an old sampler.

In the dining-room of the Francis Tuckerman Parker house is a venerable Hepplewhite sideboard, above which hangs the smiling portrait of Leverett Saltonstall, the first Mayor of Salem. The bronze and crystal chandelier is a notable family piece, as is the Duncan Phyfe table.

The
Blanchard-Archer-Smith House

Built on Federal Street about 1800 by Benjamin Blanchard, this house is noteworthy for its fine woodcarving, which probably came from the workshop of Samuel McIntire. Philip Horton Smith, architect and former owner of this house, rescued some of the mantelpieces, cornices, and trim from the Enoch Dow house on Lafayette Street when it was demolished in 1914. Authorities generally agree that this was a McIntire house, built in 1809. Later Mr. Smith installed much of the salvaged woodcarving in this Federal Street house, including the handsome mantel at the right.

When the Blanchard-Archer-Smith house was enlarged, the windows flanking the fireplace were converted into recessed bookshelves.

The panel of the living-room mantel in the Blanchard-Archer-Smith house shows a graceful handling of a sentimental theme. The group is of plaster, probably from one of McIntire's molds.

An old Pennsylvania Dutch cupboard occupies a corner of the dining-room.

This detail of the living-room mantel reveals an infectious touch of Springtime.

The drawing-room of the Blanchard-Archer-Smith house has delicate reeding on the cornices, door and window frames, and mantel. French urns and a bronze clock lend dignity to the classic fireplace.

An Adamesque mantel of unusual grace, surely worthy of McIntire, adorns the dining-room.

Salem can be particularly proud of its private collections of old china. This group of fine Canton pieces, lusterware, Delft vases, and Waterford glass decanters was formerly in THE BARSTOW-WEST HOUSE.

THE ABBOT HOUSE on Andover Street has changed hands often. A good "corner" chair and a Hepplewhite wall table grace the living-room, whose finely reeded cornice and window frames show the McIntire influence. The banjo clock fits its place of honor well. The house was built around 1800.

It has never been proven that McIntire designed the Abbot house, or that he carved the delicately reeded and festooned mantel in the living-room. It is obvious, however, that he inspired its design.

The entrance hall of the Abbot house shows the familiar architectural treatment of a steep stairway built close against the central chimney. At the stair base stands an old nail-studded leather chest.

The Sage-Webb-Wilkins House

This fine brick-end structure with four chimneys, three stories, and an attic, was built on Essex Street by Daniel Sage. Contracts for the construction have been found, but the exact date of the house is still a matter of conjecture. Sage, a Scotsman, married Deborah Silsbee, whose great-grandfather, Stephen Daniel, had built a sturdy house across the street more than a century before. Benjamin Webb was a subsequent owner of the house, which appears to date from about 1800. For almost half a century it has belonged to the Wilkins family, and it is now the home of Judge Raymond S. Wilkins.

The mantel in the parlor of the Sage-Webb-Wilkins house is the twin of one in the dining-room, except for the wide shelf, a later addition. A pair of old leather firebuckets, emblazoned "Naumkeag," flank the fireplace. To the left stand a grandmother's clock and one of three Sheraton chairs carved by McIntire.

A beautiful Aaron Willard clock ticks away in the back parlor of the Sage-Webb-Wilkins house.

One of the fine pieces in the house is this bonnet-top highboy with fan carvings and fluted pilasters.

A detail of the dining-room mantel shows it to be inspired by the McIntire precedent.

A rare and colorful lyre wall clock, by Currier & Foster of Salem, is in the dining-room.

A noble Aaron Willard grandfather's clock stands in the front parlor of the Sage-Webb-Wilkins house. Inside the door are preserved a fragment of the original bill for $70, dated October 29, 1807, and the original broadside, with instructions presumably in Willard's own hand.

A fine mahogany block-front desk stands in a recess in the rear parlor of the Sage-Webb-Wilkins house. The armchair is an old bannister-back. On the wall is a "Family Register" sampler dating from 1828.

The Rum Shop

This was built in 1800 as a sailor's tavern, and stood at the head of famous Derby Wharf. It has recently been restored, and now forms a part of the Salem Maritime National Historic Site. At present it serves as an antique shop with a certain "old curiosity shop" charm. Wooden Indians, Windsor chairs, maple desks, bird cages, ship models, chandeliers, hurricane lamps, old prints, pewter, and paintings come and go, and the interior arrangements change constantly. The present views were taken in 1949.

The ground floor of the Rum shop is filled with a fascinating miscellany, including an old tavern bar and a pedimented cabinet containing old apothecary jars. The tin chandelier is a fine one. The architectural pediment at the right, long since sold, came from the old Salem postoffice.

According to some early accounts, the second floor of the Rum shop was once used for less praiseworthy purposes than at the present time. It now serves as a salesroom for old chairs, books, and weathervanes

The Cook-Oliver House

This aristocratic house on Federal Street ushers in a series of mansions designed by Samuel McIntire at the creative peak of his career. The house was built in 1802-03, for Captain Samuel Cook, and was remodeled in 1808. The legend has been that much of the interior and exterior woodcarving in this house came from the short-lived Elias Hasket Derby mansion, considered to be McIntire's masterpiece. That noble structure was torn down early in the 19th century, and its paneling and carving was dissipated in many directions. Contemporary descriptions and McIntire's own quite dissimilar drawings for the Derby mansion indicate that the above legend is erroneous and that the Cook-Oliver house was planned by McIntire as it stands.

The fireplace in the living-room of the Cook-Oliver house is a very lovely example of McIntire's later style. Here is found one of the earliest fireplace grates in Salem, set in soapstone and flanked by handsome brasses. At the right is a delicately inlaid tambour desk, dating from the 18th century.

The spontaneity and grace of McIntire's carvings is evident in this detail of the living-room fireplace. The elongated acanthus leaf capital and the intertwining motif on the dado are both original.

The delicate carving of door and cornice in the front hall of the Cook-Oliver house is enhanced by the soft light which filters through the fan and sidelights. McIntire's gift of simplicity is eloquent here.

The Captain Jonathan Hodges House

Salem's celebrated Chestnut Street, often referred to as "The most perfect street in America," was marsh land in the town's early days, attaining its true splendor only in the early 19th century. The only McIntire house on the street is this three-story brick structure, built for Captain Hodges by Nathan Robinson in 1804. It resembles its neighbors closely, but the interior woodcarving bears the special mark of McIntire's genius. His other buildings on Chestnut Street were Hamilton Hall and the beautiful wooden South Church, destroyed by a tragic fire in 1903.

Morning sunlight adds sparkle to the center of interest of the east bedroom, a chaste fireplace with authentic brasses. A Willard clock and a John Benson marine painting are among the wall decorations.

The drawing-room of the Captain Jonathan Hodges house is formal but friendly. Its walls are covered with Chinese silver tea paper, and the curtains are of gold brocade with gilt metal cornices. An eighteen-day black and gold French clock sits under glass on the mantel shelf above a composition basket of fruit, which has been added to the chaste center panel of McIntire's fireplace.

The dining-room of the Captain Jonathan Hodges house has a Chippendale dignity. Above the fireplace is an oil painting of wild ducks by Frank W. Benson. In the corner hangs a Simon Willard banjo clock.

The dining-room is also papered in Chinese silver tea paper. The Hepplewhite sideboard is an English piece. The door frames are obviously post-McIntire additions, dating from the mid-19th century.

Another east bedroom has a very restrained mantel, accented with McIntire's subtle reeding.

The central hallway of the Captain Jonathan Hodges house is brightened by an elaborate stair rail, whose newel post (left) is carved from one single piece of wood. On the right is a detail of the upper landing.

Hamilton Hall

This dignified Assembly Hall on Chestnut Street was built in 1805 at a reputed cost of $22,000, and named for the great Federalist, Alexander Hamilton. The project of erecting a building where men and maidens danced was strongly opposed by Dr. Hopkins, minister of the South Church across the street. In one of his sermons he declaimed: "Back to back and breast to breast they are dancing their souls down to hell!" Samuel McIntire is not mentioned in early documents concerning Hamilton Hall, but his close association with leaders in the Federalist movement, as well as the workmanship and style of the structure, suggests that he was the builder.

For almost a century and a half, Hamilton Hall has been the center of Salem's social activity. Governor Christopher Gore, Commodore Bainbridge, Commander of the frigate "Constitution," and General Lafayette were all entertained here. The gilt mirrors were supposedly brought from Russia in 1809.

Many old records and letters refer to the fashionable assemblies and banquets held in Hamilton Hall. The orchestra occupied a balcony above the entrance doorway to the ballroom. Frequent mention is also made of John Remond, the colored *restaurateur,* who occupied a store on the ground floor and dispensed a very famous turtle soup each morning at eleven. He took care of the catering for generations of assemblies. The building was "modernized" in 1844, with not the best effect. In recent years the hall has been restored to its pristine beauty, largely with funds raised on "Chestnut Street Day," a memorable and infrequent occasion when the street and most of its houses are opened to the public.

The graceful ballroom is still the invariable setting for Salem's coming-out parties and assemblies.

It is in such architectural details as the mantels, lengthy pilasters, and Palladian windows that the assumption of McIntire authorship of Hamilton Hall seems so well justified.

The Pingree House

The Pingree House, built in 1804 for Captain John Gardner and designed by Samuel McIntire, is the finest brick house credited to the great carver-architect, and probably his most skillful accomplishment as a craftsman. The house was acquired by David Pingree in the 1830's and stayed for many decades in the Pingree family until it was turned over to the Essex Institute. Under the Institute's auspices it has been restored, flawlessly furnished, and opened to the public. During the Victorian era many of the McIntire wooden mantels were replaced by marble ones, but the originals were found stored in the attic, along with the decorative stair rail, and all have been restored to their original setting. The Pingree house expresses the restrained opulence which marked the homes of wealthy merchants and ship owners of Salem's great days.

As a symbol of McIntire's incomparable carving, here is a detail from the mantel in the Crowninshield Memorial Bedroom. It seems fair to assert that no American craftsman has ever surpassed him in his field.

Focal point in the front parlor of the Pingree house is a more elaborate McIntire fireplace, sparkling with white marble and carved detail. Two orange-yellow Lowestoft urns lend an appropriate accent.

McIntire's instinctive sense of design and his woodcarving skill imbue this oval fruitbasket panel with rare beauty. It is a motif which was later much abused. Above it is a glimpse of the old French calendar paper which is used throughout the front parlor.

Four Hepplewhite chairs surround a Hepplewhite card table in a corner of the front parlor. The graceful curtains are made of fine India mull in "tambour" embroidery. On the right wall hangs a girandole mirror.

The dining-room of the Pingree house is tinted a simple turquoise blue. Sheraton chairs surround the table, which holds a handsome candelabra on a French silver tray. Over the mantelpiece hangs a portrait of Timothy Fitch, by Blackburn.

The dining-room fireplace (left) is designed in a simpler mood, and is embellished with graceful bell metal andirons.

The front and back parlors of the Pingree house have identical fireplaces. This one, in the back parlor, carries three fine Lowestoft vases. Above it is one panel of the old French wallpaper, designed by Fragonard *fils* in 1808, which belonged to the Essex Institute. Each panel represents a different month of the year. The coloring is deep blue on gold. A Lowestoft tea set rests invitingly on the table. On the floor is an Aubusson rug.

The Crowninshield Memorial Bedroom, in the northeast corner, is the most colorful room in the Pingree house. Its windows are hung with blue and apricot damask draperies, as is its handsome "marriage bed."

This view of the Crowninshield Memorial Bedroom shows a pleasant wall group built around an old banjo clock, and provides a glimpse across the central hall.

The wheat sheaf is probably the most individual, the most personal, of all of McIntire's carved devices. One can distinguish the handiwork of the master from that of his imitators by a comparative study of this motif alone. This brilliant detail is from the fireplace of the Crowninshield Room.

Above the fireplace in the Crowninshield Memorial Bedroom is a painting of the launching of the ship "Fame" in Salem Harbor, painted in 1812 by George Ropes. This was a Crowninshield vessel.

The furniture in the northeast bedroom of the Pingree house is grouped with admirable balance. At the left a Chippendale mirror hangs over the serpentine-front bureau. In the corner is an American highboy.

The chaste fireplace of the northeast bedroom is enlivened with blue Delft jars and brass candlesticks. At the right is a painted candle screen. The walls in this room are peach colored, the draperies blue.

The southwest bedroom of the Pingree house, known as the Francis Shaw Memorial Room, is finished in robin's egg blue. Above its simple mantel is a gilt framed Salem mirror, flanked by Botticelli prints and exquisite crystal candelabras. The chair is in the French Chippendale style, with a Chinese back.

The silk draperies and bed hangings in the Shaw Memorial Room are blue, embroidered with small red roses. By the fireplace is a Martha Washington armchair with curved back, upholstered in horsehair.

Detail of the French porcelain clock by Lepère which sits in the front parlor of the Pingree house.

Two English bronze and crystal candelabra on the Shaw Room mantel shimmer with highlights.

On the third floor of the Pingree house is the Boy's Bedroom, whose low windows and ceiling give it a more informal air. The blue *toile de Jouy* curtains are from a design by Thomas Jefferson. A delicate Windsor chair from Maine stands next to the old Queen Anne card table.

The walls of the Boy's Room are covered with old French scenic paper from the "Banks of the Rhine" and "Venetian Scenes" series, making lively background for old books, pitchers, and ivory chessmen

The
Chapman-Davis-Sanders House

On Summer Street in Salem, where Samuel McIntire built his own unassuming home, is an unusual house, originally built by John Chapman in 1715, and extensively altered by Captain Tobias Davis in 1805. The handsome woodwork is from McIntire's time. The house is now in the possession of Richard D. Sanders. The 18th-century armchair shown in these views was made in Marblehead. A carved Chinese table and an American Chippendale chair flank the small sofa.

The living-room fireplace in the Chapman-Davis-Sanders house projects into the room, flanked by a window on either side. A handsome set of bronze and crystal candelabra brightens the mantel shelf.

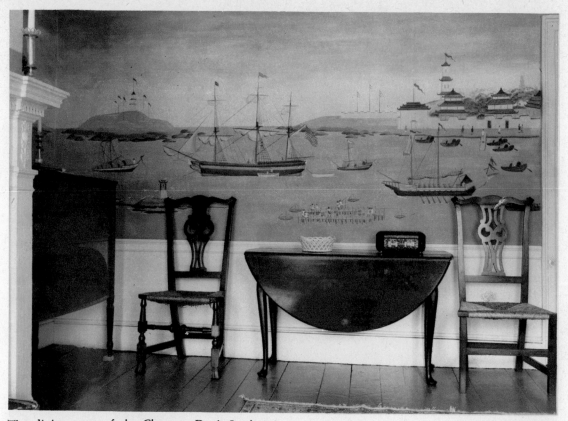

The dining-room of the Chapman-Davis-Sanders house is decorated with wall paintings by the Salem artist, Philip Von Saltza, in the manner of early paintings, showing American ships in Chinese ports.

The dining-room mantel is presumably by McIntire. Above it is a painting of the ship "John."

A graceful Sheraton sideboard with reeded posts and doors fits well in the dining-room alcove.

THE CLIFFORD CROWNINSHIELD HOUSE on Washington Square, built in 1804-06, is another authenticated McIntire house. In 1809 the house became the property of Captain James Devereux who commanded the ship "Franklin" of Boston, the first ship to go into Japan and return.

1

In the living-room of the Clifford Crowninshield house is a fluted mantel reflecting McIntire's later style. The central panel contains a carved trophy of musical instruments of most unusual design.

The finest piece of furniture in this house is a superb claw-foot, block-front desk with shell.

A detail of the mantel in the northwest chamber shows McIntire's simpler style and mouldings.

THE BUTMAN-WATERS HOUSE, built on Cambridge Street in 1806-07 for Thomas Butman, is another verified work of Samuel McIntire. The living-room fireplace and cornice bear his sure stamp.

McIntire's familiar carved basket of fruit is more generously laden here than in the Pingree house. This became an immensely popular motif in the 19th century and was added to innumerable mantels.

The mantel of the Butman-Waters house offers a good chance to distinguish between ornament carved from wood and plaster ornament applied and painted over. The garland clearly falls in the latter category.

THE BACALL HOUSE, built on Federal Street near the turn of the 18th century, has a cheerful living-room fireplace, flanked by bookshelves. A brass kettle and a Normandy jug brighten the foreground.

A mahogany and gilt Georgian mirror with a phoenix reflects a pewter-laden dining-room mantel.

A mahogany veneer Sheraton secretary holds a shelf of books behind diamond-paned doors.

The Solomon Towne House

One of the earliest of the dignified mansions on Chestnut Street to be built by a sea captain is this three-story dwelling with a classic Doric portico. This was built in 1810 by Captain Solomon Towne, who commanded the "Galatea" and who died on the coast of Sumatra in 1835. A late afternoon sun brushes across the slashed clapboards, granite steps and sill, and the brick sidewalk, all hallmarks of Salem's most famous street. Every few years the street is roped off for a day, old costumes are brought forth, houses are thrown open to the public and the picture of Salem a century ago is brought back to life.

The library fireplace in the Solomon Towne house is reminiscent of Samuel McIntire, who died in 1811, but whose influence survived for generations.

The dining-room of the Solomon Towne house is dignified and cheerful. The table, in the style of Duncan Phyfe, has a complement of graceful chairs. A secretary of the same period stands in the corner.

The dining-room sideboard, a beautiful Hepplewhite restoration, is the keynote of a well-balanced wall arrangement.

A second-floor mantel in the Solomon Towne house is carved with the familiar wheat sheaf and that proud emblem of the Federal period, the American eagle. Two china dogs also stand watch.

A graceful bow-front table stands in a corner of the dining-room, under a gilt convex mirror.

Another bedroom fireplace is framed with patterend tile and a reeded mantel.

The living-room of the Solomon Towne house reflects both comfort and good taste.

In the corner niche of the living-room is a rare highboy, a family piece from Philadelphia.

Another fine mantelpiece of the time and style of Samuel McIntire is found in THE GRACE CHURCH PARISH HOUSE, on Essex Street, which was probably built about 1810 by John Cabot.

THE SANDERS-SALTONSTALL HOUSE, a large and imposing two-family house at the western end of Chestnut Street, was built by Thomas Sanders for his two daughters, who married Leverett and Nathaniel Saltonstall respectively. The eastern wing, built for the daughter who married Leverett Saltonstall, later Mayor of Salem, contains this spiral staircase, probably the finest in Salem.

A commodious double drawing-room extends through the eastern wing of the Sanders-Saltonstall house.

The graceful spiral continues up for two flights. These two views are taken on the second-floor landing.

The western half of THE SANDERS-SALTONSTALL HOUSE, built for the bride of Nathaniel Saltonstall, is furnished with many unique pieces, among them this old family barometer.

The dining-room of the western half is furnished with fine period pieces, including a crystal chandelier of Waterford glass, dating from 1750, which was formerly the property of the Duchess of St. Albans.

A restored spiral staircase of wide sweep rises up in the hall.

A close-up of the dining-room mantel reveals classic figures on both sides of the corner.

THE SILSBEE-CLARK HOUSE, built on Washington Square between 1812 and 1820, contains a small treasury of furniture and *objets d'art*. The double drawing-room is divided by a wide fan-lighted elliptical arch, an architectural motif which became immensely popular later in the 19th century. The rear half of the room is now used as a doctor's office. On its walls hang two Benjamin West portraits.

The dining-room of the Silsbee-Clark house is decorated with a fine picture paper, made by Zuber of Alsace, representing the arctic, temperate and tropical zones. The sideboard is a superb Hepplewhite.

In the drawing-room of the Silsbee-Clark house is a rare and beautiful sofa, believed to have been carved by the versatile Samuel McIntire for a house he designed. It is upholstered in dark red brocade.

The Pickering-Northey House

Two imposing twin houses were built on Chestnut Street in 1814-15 for Henry and John Pickering by Jabez Smith, Salem's post-McIntire master builder. The western half (right), known as the Pickering-Northey house, is said to be the setting for the reception held for President Jackson when he visited Salem in 1833. Here lived William E. Northey, celebrated as a maker of fine ship models, many of which are now in the Peabody Museum.

The drawing-room of the Pickering-Northey house is furnished with traditional Chippendale and Hepplewhite pieces. Over the door leading to the dining-room are two Northey ship models.

The vogue of the stone mantel was beginning at the time the Pickering-Northey house was built. This example in the drawing-room is carved from dark grey marble. Over it hangs an old family portrait. The andirons and brass-trimmed serpentine fender are old pieces, as are the colorful Chinese jars.

Many Chestnut Street houses contain collections of Oriental objects brought back by their early seafaring owners. Against the background of an old sampler, here is china, pewter, ivory, lusterware, and carved wood from the far corners of the world, assembled in the Pickering-Northey house.

A pair of Sheffield candelabra flank the flower pots in the sunny dining-room window.

An elliptically arched opening frames the drawing-room. Chairs are early Queen Anne.

THE PICKERING-MACK-VER PLANCK HOUSE, eastern half of the double structure, has several fine
fireplaces, among them this one of white Italian marble. Above it hangs a portrait of Major General
Jacob Brown, secretary to Alexander Hamilton and commander of the land forces in the War of 1812.

The drawing-room is distinguished by a white marble mantel and a near-Victorian chandelier.

In the dining-room is an Empire grey mantelpiece holding two early mahogany knife boxes.

The central hall is partially lighted by the side lights and fanlight of the graceful front door.

The dining-room is architecturally imposing. The old sideboard is in the Empire tradition.

The entrance hall of the Pickering-Mack-Ver Planck house follows a classic Salem pattern. The staircase springs gracefully to the second floor. The old grandfather's clock was built for Major General Brown.

The
Captain George Nichols House

Typical of the well-groomed three-story Federal mansion which is the essence of Chestnut Street, the Captain George Nichols house is an eloquent spokesman for the good taste of the Federal period. It was built in 1816, while the McIntire influence was still strong. Its classic entranceway bespeaks both charm and dignity.

The woodwork in the dining-room is painted a delicate grey, a pleasant foil for the Sheraton sideboard and chairs. Contemporary paintings by Jacob Getler Smith and Waldo Pierce harmonize with the setting.

The drawing-room of the Captain George Nichols house retains a reposeful elegance. The paper and woodwork are soft green, and the hangings are an attenuated apricot. At the right is an old gilt mirror.

The drawing-room mantelpiece is very
much in the McIntire tradition, even to
the skillful cutting of the wheat sheaf.

On the mantel shelf are two interesting
lamps by Messenger, of Liverpool.

A door in the drawing-room of the Captain George Nichols house leads to a spacious and inviting library paneled in natural pine. By the doorway is a Sheraton "fancy" chair.

A detail of the sensitive mantelpiece in the east chamber shows the enlivening contrast of an old oil lamp, a framed silhouette, and a marine print.

The west chamber of the Captain George Nichols house is a study in comfort, restraint, and the skillful use of fabrics.

The simple fireplace in the west chamber is ornamented with carved figures. Above it hangs a painting by Philip Von Saltza.

The
Dudley Pickman House

The Dudley Pickman house is probably the largest on Chestnut Street, extending to the rear in successive wings. It was built by the master builder, Jabez Smith, between 1817 and 1821.

The drawing-room of the Dudley Pickman house has impressive dimensions. A wall with a wide door once divided this into front and back drawing-rooms. This was removed in 1900, creating one handsome room 50 feet long.

Two nearly identical fireplaces occur in the drawing-room. Each has a mantelpiece of dark carved mahogany with orange-yellow marble facing, and an old Italian landscape painting as an overmantel. The walls in this room are pale green, the hangings gold brocade.

The dining-room of the Dudley Pickman house is enlivened with a grey scenic wallpaper which harmonizes with grey blue hangings. The 18th-century mahogany sideboard is an original English piece.

The dining-room is spacious and formal, almost on the ambassadorial scale. Some of the furnishings are reproductions of Chippendale pieces.

The dining-room fireplace, flanked by two Corinthian pilasters, has great dignity. The grey marble mantel is delicately carved, as is the graceful spray above the mirrow. The woodwork is a warm pale grey.

The Pickering Dodge-Shreve House

The Pickering Dodge-Shreve house probably possesses the thickest walls and the most imposing doorway on Chestnut Street. Built in 1822-23 by David Lord, another master builder, the house provides a shining example of the acquisitive nature of Salem shipmasters and merchants. It contains three marble mantels brought over from Italy, furniture from England, and much china from the Orient. Pickering Dodge had a weakness for marble mantels and, when he traveled to Italy with his friends Dudley Pickman and Captain Charles Sanders (Chestnut Street residents all), each of them brought back one or more mantelpieces for his own house.

This fireplace in the Pickering Dodge-Shreve house is perhaps the most ornate of the marble importations. Two graceful caryatids support the mantel shelf and a head of Medusa writhes with snakes in the center.

The marble mantel in the east parlor was installed about 75 years ago to replace an earlier and less handsome one. Above it hangs a portrait of James Silver, Commander of the ship "Leander" and ancestor of the present owner. Captain Silver had the distinction of being almost buried alive at sea. Apparently dead in the tropics from smallpox, his crew was preparing his body for burial on shipboard when a thunderstorm interrupted them. After the storm they were startled to see the captain move uneasily. He was freed from his shroud, survived the smallpox, and died in his Salem home many years later.

Above a tambour desk in the front parlor of the Pickering Dodge-Shreve house is this harmonious group of gracious objects, among them an 18th-century gilt mirror, Lowestoft vases, and an old flower print.

The classic marble mantel in the front parlor is original with the house. On its broad shelf repose two gilt and crystal five-branched candelabra, a Chinese bowl, and two *famille rose* plates. A corner of the room, including the group illustrated on the opposite page, is reflected in the old convex mirror.

The rear parlor of the Pickering Dodge-Shreve house contains several choice pieces besides the Italian mantel, notably a French pastoral painting, an Empire sofa, and a Sheraton secretary.

An old mirror provides a reflected glimpse of the mantel. At the right is a needlepoint candle screen.

In the dining-room is a fine Sheraton secretary with an ancestral collection of Nanking china.

The spacious central hallway of the Pickering Dodge-Shreve house is given the illusion of even greater scale by the child's miniature ladder-back chair. The deeply cut frame of the door, with ornamental corner squares, is from a later period, a first hint of the Victorian era to come.

A stately looking glass increases the impression of luminous space in the front parlor of the Pickering Dodge-Shreve house. Lace curtains of delicate design adorn the windows. A five-branch crystal candelabra occupies the center of interest in front of the mirror.

THE HUMPHREY DEVEREUX HOUSE on Chestnut Street is a noteworthy example of the taste of the Federal period. The spacious drawing-room has, as its center of interest, a McIntire-designed mantel. Above it hangs a painting of Derby Wharf by the Salem artist, Philip Little. At the left is an unusual American-made cabinet, lacquered in black and gold in China.

The central panel of the living-room mantel reveals McIntire in his more elaborate mood. But with all the rich mouldings, the portrait bust, the urns, and the scrolls, he achieves a restful balance.

The fine proportions and judicious detail of the ultimate McIntire mantel can be observed in this view of the living-room mantel in the Humphrey Devereux house. At the left is a piecrust-top table.

A detail of the fireplace reveals symmetrical dolphins and varied maritime insignia.

On the marble dining-room fireplace stands a clock by Eli Terry and Chinese jade screens.

THE BUTLER HOUSE. Pickering Dodge began the construction of Chestnut Street's only triple house in 1828. He died before it was finished, and the work was carried on by his son-in-law, John Fiske Allen. The western wing is handsomely furnished with early American pieces.

The drawing-room mantel, carved from grey Italian marble, is embellished with French figurines and candelabra with tear-drop crystals. Above is a flower painting by Philip Von Saltza.

The sideboard shimmers with silver and carries a pair of old walnut knife boxes from France. On the wall is one of a pair of old silver candle sconces against grey and white wallpaper.

The Oriental influence is strong in the library, whose walls are covered with Chinese grass cloth. Over the mantel is a decorative framed silk scarf from Indo-China. The woodwork is a soft green.

Above the Hepplewhite sideboard hangs a painting by the gifted Salem artist, Philip Von Saltza.

THE VON SALTZA HOUSE strikes a different note in Salem interiors, since most of its furnishings consist of ancestral pieces brought over from Sweden. This 18th-century clock, flanked by gilded dolphins and capped with a lyre, is a striking example. Beneath it stands a 17th-century silver canister.

The living-room of the Von Saltza house, built about 1830, is furnished with 18th-century Swedish pieces of French inspiration. They came originally from an old estate on the Baltic shore.

In the living-room stands a Louis XV three-drawer marquetry chest, under a colorful still-life.

The dining-room displays armorial Lowestoft plates, made in China for Swedish collectors.

THE KITTREDGE-ROGERS HOUSE, built about 1832, faces Hamilton Hall on Cambridge Street and contains a remarkable collection of old furniture. In this view of the west parlor, every piece, from the rare grandmother's clock down to the smallest ornament on the maple desk, is authentic.

The dining-room of the Kittredge-Rogers house is filled with interesting pieces. At the left is a small burl walnut highboy. Over the Hepplewhite sideboard hangs a fine Chippendale mirror. Old glass flasks silhouette themselves against the window panes.

A William and Mary walnut highboy stands under a family portrait in the living-room of the Kittredge-Rogers house. On the mantel shelf are old French oil lamps with crystal pendants. The Liverpool pitcher on the shelf has a design in orange-red which is reflected in the rug and the *toile de Jouy* curtains.

The west parlor of the Kittredge-Rogers house is abundantly furnished with ancestral pieces. The secretary, serving table, highboy, family portrait, and old framed samplers all come from one collection.

Over the living-room desk are two brass candlesticks, a crystal candelabra, and a gilt mirror.

The west parlor fireplace is rich with Federal ornament, including an impressive convex mirror.

The Nathaniel West House

This imposing Chestnut Street dwelling was the home of Captain Nathaniel West and his wife, the daughter of Elias Hasket Derby. It stood originally in Peabody, but after a divorce which rather shattered the community, Captain West moved the house to Salem as a home for his daughter, Martha. The moving, which took place in 1824, was accomplished by separating the house in two parts and towing it by teams of oxen. The portico and gate posts were added by the present owner, Stephen W. Phillips, in 1912.

All of the mantels in the Nathaniel West house are unusual, but the richly carved example in the library, ornamented with flowers, fruit baskets, and horns of plenty, is unique in its conception and detail.

The fireboard of the library fireplace in the Nathaniel West house consists of a painting on canvas by George Ropes, of Salem, dated 1805. The influence of Claude Lorrain is evident in the landscape.

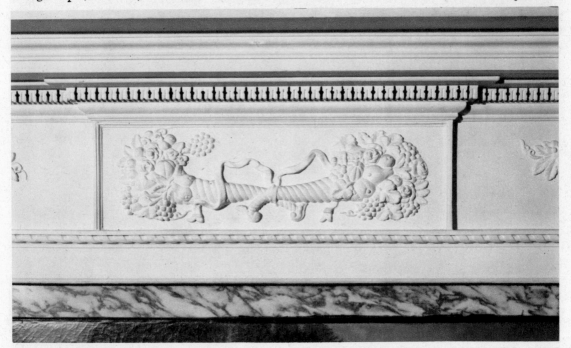

The center panel of this mantel is filled with two unconventional cornucopias, skillfully carved.

The harvest motif is emphasized in the drawing-room mantel, which appears to be of later date.

The drawing-room mantel develops the grape-vine theme and initiates free standing columns.

In one of the upstairs bedrooms is an even richer mantel whose archetrave is carved in a rhythmic series of leaf and fruit patterns.

In the dining-room, a comparatively recent addition to the Nathaniel West house, is a glass-enclosed cupboard filled with family pieces of Canton china in various rich colors, made between 1820 and 1856.

THE RANTOUL HOUSE. Until two years ago an old house on Winter Street gave one of the best pictures of mid-19th-century *décor* in Salem. This house, the home of the Rantoul family for almost a century, contained family pieces ranging from early Dutch-back chairs to Victorian sofas.

Another view of the drawing-room in the Rantoul house shows an Empire sofa, table, and chair, a window crowned by French blue brocade lambrequins, and a fine mantel carved from grey Italian marble.

THE DALAND MANSION. The Victorian Room in the Essex Institute once served as the drawing-room of the Daland mansion, built in 1849. The handsome crystal chandelier was formerly in the Brooks mansion near Medford. On the table stands a Rogers group, flanked by two rare "transparencies." The room has dignity and poise, but holds a hint that two centuries of good taste are drawing to a close.

THE PEIRCE-NICHOLS HOUSE

INDEX